Parenting
(14 Gospel Principles That Can Radically Change Your Family)
Discussion Guide:
Parents Small Group Discussion Questions

Andrew Yoon Joo Lee

Version 1.0 – May, 2022

Copyright © 2022 by Yoon Joo Lee

Quotations are from *Parenting: 14 Gospel Principles That Can Radically Change Your Family* by Paul David Tripp (page numbers are indicated at the end of each quotation).

All rights reserved, including the right of reproduction in whole or in part in any form.

Table of Contents

Introduction 4

How to Use This Guide 7

Chapter 1 – Calling 10

Chapter 2 - Grace 14

Chapter 3 - Law 18

Chapter 4 - Inability 20

Chapter 5 - Identity 24

Chapter 6 - Process 28

Chapter 7 - Lost 34

Chapter 8 - Authority 38

Chapter 9 - Foolishness 42

Chapter 10 - Character 46

Chapter 11 - False Gods 52

Chapter 12 - Control 56

Chapter 13 - Rest 60

Chapter 14 - Mercy 66

About the Author 71

Introduction

Parenting is hard, and everyone knows it. People say it's the most challenging thing we do as human beings. It's also a sacred calling from God. But how much support do you have on your journey of parenting?

Do you have other parent friends with whom you can share the joys and struggles, encourage one another and find the support you need as a parent? Do you have guides that show you a clear picture of what parenting is really about according to God's grand plan of salvation?

Paul Tripp's Parenting: 14 Gospel Principles That Can Radically Change Your Family is one of the best guides that provides parents of the roadmap of parenting as God intended it to be. It shows the readers how the gospel works in action in the lives of the children through parents who humbly let the gospel work in their lives.

Reading it will be helpful. Better yet, talking about it after reading it with other parents, reflecting on your parenting journey and practices based on your learnings, and applying the gospel principles to your family with the encouragement and prayer from other parent friends can change your family.

Parenting Discussion Guide was written with that aim in my mind. I used this with the youth parents when I served as a youth pastor at my church, and I have been blessed with real change and growth in my family as well as by seeing other parents finding encouragement and hope in their parenting journey. Such fruit is possible only through Jesus apart from whom we can do nothing. So, rather than trying to make change happen on our own, we need to find God's real work in ourselves and join Him in that. This guide will help you and your group do just that.

PARENTING DISCUSSION GUIDE

When was your last time being in a small group of parents and thinking you were deeply enjoying the time together with others and feeling like you were actually getting the help and support you need as a parent?

If you are like me (and if you have an experience of being in a small group), you probably had a variety of kinds of small group experiences. Some are absolutely engaging; discussions are deep, honest, and vulnerable, and you feel that God is alive and active among the group. Others are not so great; conversations, if existent, are mostly about facts, and often one person dominates the discussion and turns it into a sermon or devotion.

What do you think makes a great small group discussion? What enables people of God to go deeper into the journey of parenting and of discipleship that bears tangible fruit in life rather than simply gain more knowledge without any change in life? There might be many different answers. I believe it starts with the leader. When the leader of the group first engages in her of his journey of parenting genuinely and then honestly shares it with others, others are encouraged to do the same. Actually, to be more accurate, it is not that the leader must share first every single time the group meets; rather, whoever shares first happens to lead the group spiritually in that moment.

A great small group experience is not just about the transmission of knowledge but also about the transformation of souls; and it needs to start with an actual person in the particularities of her or his life. And when such particular story is shared with others, suddenly God becomes real.

God is always on the move; in the world, in the church, in the society, in the workplace and school, in the neighborhood, in our families, in my heart. What is He doing right now? What is God doing in His grand salvation story of humanity? And locating my story to that Big Story, what is God doing in me? Around me?

Through me? Answering these questions, I believe, is one of the main purposes of small group discussions.

As we discover what God is doing in our lives, on our journey of parenting, and in our heart, we're invited to share our journey with each other. And as we share that with others in fierce honesty as much as possible, grounded in the security of God's never-ending love and mercy, we are encouraged to obey God's will and bear fruit.

What else makes a great small group discussion? Good questions do. I would argue that even more important than the right answers are good questions. Moreover, God delights and uses our questions; not just those intellectual questions but also those that are visceral, those that matter to you deeply and personally.

I hope and pray that you will find the questions in this guide to be an invitation to God's real work in you soaking you with His fatherly love and mercy; that you would be able to say 'yes' to the invitation and follow and obey Him as His tool of rescuing and transforming the lives of your children, upheld by others through sharing the real journey together.

       Andrew Yoon Joo Lee

PARENTING DISCUSSION GUIDE

How to Use This Guide

This guide book is for small group discussions on Parenting: 14 Gospel Principles That Can Radically Change Your Family, written by Paul Tripp. You can also use it as a couple with your spouse or on your own though it may not be ideal. If you choose to do it alone, I recommend you keep a journal and share your reflections and your spiritual journey through it with others. There is something really powerful about sharing our authentic journey in Jesus with other human beings.

The chapters in this guide are directly from the book, Parenting, with the same chapter numbers and titles. The participants are to be expected to have read the corresponding chapter before joining the small group discussions. If fourteen sessions feel too long, you can divide them into two series.

The recommended duration of each small group discussion is one hour and a half, but it can be shorter or longer depending on the size of your group and the dynamic of the discussion. I suggest that, instead of going through every single question one by one, you lump two or three questions together and ask if people want to discuss any of them. Think ahead of time how to group questions considering the flow of the discussion. Separate the application questions since they intentionally get more personal, and give enough time for people to think and share.

One amazing way to boost engagement is for every member (or some members) to take turns in facilitating the discussions each week. On the first week, the leader can model facilitation and ask everyone else to sign up for facilitation for the remaining sessions. Whoever is scheduled to lead the next week will get to engage more deeply with the book and her or his reflection. Also, different facilitation styles tend to bring out different parts of the members, resulting in a richer and more diverse experience.

Make sure to leave some time at the end to spend time together in prayer.

It is also a good idea to have a potluck gathering in the beginning or after all the sessions are finished or between the two series.

These are my suggestions, but I am sure that there are also million other ways parents small groups can thrive. So, pray and ask the Holy Spirit and follow His guidance!

May God work mightily and wondrously among your small group and in your family!

PARENTING DISCUSSION GUIDE

Chapter 1 – Calling

1. Which of the stories from the first several pages of this chapter do you identify with the most? Or if you don't identify as much, how is your parenting story different?

2. The calling as a parent is "one of the most significant callings that could ever be laid in the lap of a human being" (p.24). How do you feel when you hear that?

Parents As Treasure Hunters

3. Tripp says, "Everything you do and say in your life, every choice that you make, and everything you decide to invest in is a reflection of a system of internalized values in your heart" (p.24-25). What does he mean? Do you agree?

"Parenting is either a thing of the highest treasure to you, and that is demonstrated in your choices, words, and actions every day, or it's not" (p.25).

4. "Parents who are too controlled by possessions (houses, cars, lawns, furniture, artwork, etc.) tend to be so busy acquiring, maintaining, financing, and protecting their possessions that they have way too little time to invest in their children in the way God intended" (p.25-26). Do physical things get in the way of, or create needless tension in, your parenting? In what ways?

5. How has the value of career success impacted your commitment to the work that God has called you to as parents? In what ways?

6. Do ministry decisions and commitments make it hard for you to faithfully do your work as a parent? In what ways?

7. What are some tangible and specific ways you can declutter your life from the distractions and idols (possessions, career success, ministry, etc.) so you can refocus your life on your calling as a parent? What help or support do you need from your family, church, and people around you in order for you to make this change in your life?

Here's How God Values Parents

8. Read the passages below. Where does God stop you? Why?

> Hear, O Israel; The Lord our God, the Lord is one. You shall love the Lord your God with all your heart and with all your soul and with all your might. And these words that I command you today shall be on your heart. You shall teach them diligently to your children, and shall talk of them when you sit in your house, and when you walk by the way, and when you lie down, and when you rise. You shall bind them as a sign on your hand, and they shall be as frontlets between your eyes. You shall write them on the doorposts of your house and on your gates. (Deut. 6:4–9)

> When your son asks you in time to come, "What is the meaning of the testimonies and the statutes and the rules that the Lord our God has commanded you?" then you shall say to your son, "We were Pharaoh's slaves in Egypt. And the Lord brought us out of Egypt with a mighty hand. And the Lord showed signs

and wonders, great and grievous, against Egypt and against Pharaoh and all his household, before our eyes. And he brought us out from there, that he might bring us in and give us the land that he swore to give our fathers." (Deut. 6:20–23)

"Your work as a parent is a thing of extreme value because God has designed that you would be a principal, consistent, and faithful tool in his hands for the purpose of creating God-consciousness and God-submission in your children. ... The most important thing that a child could ever learn about is the existence, character, and plan of God" (p.30).

9. Tripp says that "we should root all the rules and beliefs that we give our children not only in the existence of God, but in the things that he has, in grace, done for us" (p.31) and "Blow your child away with God's patience, mercy, and love." What are some specific ways we can do this? Can you share any examples from your own life or from other people around you?

PARENTING DISCUSSION GUIDE

Chapter 2 - Grace

Principle: God never calls you to a task without giving you what you need to do it. He never sends you without going with you.

Discussion Questions:

1. What do you think are some of the most important things needed for consistent, faithful, patient, loving, and effective parenting?

"There is nothing more important to consistent, faithful, patient, loving, and effective parenting than to understand what God has given you in the grace of his Son, the Lord Jesus Christ ... Understanding God's grace will change you, and as it changes you, it will change the way you relate to and parent your children" (p.34).

2. What does Paul Tripp mean by past grace, future grace, and present grace? Can you share some examples of the present grace you experience in the last couple of weeks?

3. God calls unable people to do important things. What are some

PARENTING DISCUSSION GUIDE

examples of this in the Bible? In our world? Why does God call unable people?

"God calls unable people to do important things so that he will get the glory and not them. He isn't working so that your life as a parent would be easy, predictable, and free from struggle. He calls you to do the impossible so that in your search for help, you would find more than help—you would find him" (p.35-36).

4. What are the other benefits, especially for the children, of unable parents as opposed to parents who think that they are able?

5. When do you feel most discouraged or helpless or lonely as a parent? Can you share any examples from the past or the present? How can we remember in those moments that God is with us and in us?

"Here is the single redemptive reality, right here, right now, that makes parenting possible: God in you! *... This God who has the ability to do things that are way beyond your ability to conceive, who has perfect wisdom and unlimited strength, right now lives inside of you" (p.38).*

6. Tripp says, "God's grace works to open your eyes to see yourself as a parent accurately" (p.38). How might you be more like your children than unlike them in their struggles?

7. Tripp also says, "God's grace frees you from having to deny your weaknesses" (p.39). Have you experienced this in your life? Can you share briefly?

"As a parent you do not ever need to fear knowing yourself, you do not have to fear being known by those around you, and you do not have to fear being exposed as less than perfect because there is nothing that could ever be known or exposed about you as a parent that hasn't already been covered by the blood of Jesus" (p.40).

8. What does Tripp mean by the sentences below, and what are some examples of them whether from your own life or from other people's stories?

- God's grace rescues you from you. (p.40)
- God's grace grows and changes you as a parent. (p.41)
- God's grace works to make your heart tender. (p.42)
- God's grace liberates you from the prison of regret. (p.43)

… PARENTING DISCUSSION GUIDE

Chapter 3 - Law

Principle: Your children need God's law, but you cannot ask the law to do what only grace can accomplish.

Discussion Questions:

1. Tripp says, "If rules and regulations had the power to change the heart and life of your child, rescuing your child from himself and giving him a heart of submission and faith, Jesus would have never needed to come!" (p.49) What is your response to this statement?

2. What are some benefits and purposes of God's law?

3. What are some weaknesses of the law mentioned?

"This is what every parent of every child needs to understand: the law does a very good job of exposing your child's sin, but it has no power whatsoever to deliver your child from it" (p.51).

4. Do you see both the benefits and weaknesses of the law playing out if your family life with your children? What are some examples?

PARENTING DISCUSSION GUIDE

5. What are some of your own laws you tend to idolize and then make yourself captive and in bondage by? In what ways do you need to be rescued from yourself?

6. What are some examples of opportunities of "preaching the gospel" we can do in our everyday life to our children?

7. Have you ever let your children see you seeking and receiving God's grace when you need it? How might it look like for you to do that today?

"And if we are going to teach our children to run to Jesus daily, we must run to Jesus daily as well. If we want our children to be sad in the face of the sin of their hearts and hands, we must mourn our sin as parents as well. You see, it is only as we are willing to confess that we are more like than unlike our children, that we ourselves need parenting every day, that we will be parents in need of a father's grace who will again and again lead our children to the grace of the Father" (p.56-58)

Chapter 4 - Inability

Principle: Recognizing what you are unable to do is essential to good parenting.

Discussion Questions:

1. Tripp shares a story of a mom hurling accusations and threats to her little boy to change him. Have you seen similar things? Have you been part of such scenes in your life?

2. Tripp says, "you have no power whatsoever to change your child" (p.60). What is your initial response to that statement? How do you feel about it?

3. How is exercising your authority as a parent humbly as God's agent different from trying to change your children by human power? Can you think of some examples?

"If any human being possessed the power to create lasting change in any other human being, again, Jesus would not have had to come! The incarnation, life, death, and resurrection of Jesus stand as clear historical evidence that human power for change does not exist. The reason God went to such an extreme and elaborate extent in controlling the events of history so that at

PARENTING DISCUSSION GUIDE

just the right time his Son would come and do for us what we could not do ourselves, is because there was no other way" (p.60-61).

Power Tools

4. What are some "fear tactics" and threats other parents or you use to try to create change in your children? Why are threats only temporarily effective and unable to create internal heart change?

5. What are some "reward tactics" other parents or you use to try to create change in your children? Why does reward tactics fall short of creating lasting change in children?

"Change is about learning what is right, acknowledging that it is right, confessing that you have been wrong, committing to a new way of living, and seeking the help you need to do it. None of these things have happened inside Josh, because his parents sadly succumbed to the temptation to opt for control rather than to give themselves to the hard, exhausting, and often discouraging work of being tools of change in the hands of the only One who can produce it" (p.66-67).

6. How do parents use shame and guilt to try to change children? Do you remember your parents doing it to you when you were little? How might you be using shame and guilt to your children whether consciously or unconsciously?

"Like all tools of parental control, guilt and shame have a short-term positive harvest and a long-term negative legacy. At some point every child quits being moved by guilt and begins to get tired of being put down. At some point children begin to understand the dynamics of their relationship with you. At some point, even though they cannot verbalize it, children begin to understand the difference between control and patient love. They begin to see the difference between you using old tools to get them to do something and you lovingly being God's tool to help them be something. At some point they begin to distance themselves from you in order to protect themselves from the guilt and shame that often seems to come when you are near" (p.68-69)

7. How is our heavenly Father different from human parents who use power tools - fear, reward, shame - to control their children?

8. What is the good news for us, powerless parents? What hope do we have if we indeed have no power to create change in our children?

"God is with you. He wants what is best for you and your children, and no one but he has the power to produce it. He has not placed the burden of change on your shoulders because he would not require you to do what you cannot do. God has simply called you as a parent to be a humble and faithful tool of change in the lives of your children. And for that there is moment by *moment by moment grace"* (p.70).

9. What does it mean for you personally today to rest in God's power to change your children in His way at His timing instead of anxiously grabbing the ineffective tools of delusional power? How would that look for you tangibly these coming weeks?

Chapter 5 - Identity

Principle: If you are not resting as a parent in your identity in Christ, you will look for identity in your children.

Discussion Questions:

1. Does Sally and Jamie's story at the beginning of the chapter sound familiar to you? Do you know any similar stories either from people around you or from your personal experiences?

The Identity Quest

2. Tripp says, "If you are not resting in your vertical identity, you will look horizontally, searching to find yourself and your reason for living in something in the creation" (p.76). What are some horizontal identities you tend to fall into seeking more than others?

3. What does getting one's identity from her or his children look like? What does it look like in your life? Why is it a bad idea?

So How Do You Know?

"How do you know if you're putting your identity on the shoulders of your children? ... Here are five sure indications" (p.79, 80). Read the questions below and answer the questions that seem the

PARENTING DISCUSSION GUIDE

most significant to you:

4. Too much focus on success. "Could it be that you want your children to succeed too much because you *need* them to succeed? Could it be that your children are beginning to break under the heavy load of your expectations?" (p.80)

5. Too much concern about reputation. "Could it be that your reputation as a parent means too much to you? Could it be that what others think of your children is too important to you?" (p.81)

6. Too great a desire for control. Could it be that your desire for success has caused you to exercise a level of control that actually is in the way of your child's growth and development? development? Could it be that your anxiety as a parent comes from the fact that you are trying to exercise control over things you don't have the power to control?" (p.81)

7. Too much emphasis on *doing* rather than *being*. Could it be that the achievements that you want your children to produce have kept you from focusing on the things that they desperately need but cannot produce? Could it be that the focus on physical, social, and educational accomplishments has kept you from focusing on their hearts?" (p.82)

8. Too much temptation to make it personal. Could it be that tension has been caused in your relationship to your children because you have tended to personalize what is not personal? Could it be that your desire to get things from your children has

caused you to take personal offense at things that are not personal?" (p.84)

PARENTING DISCUSSION GUIDE

Chapter 6 - Process

Principle: You must be committed as a parent to long-view parenting because change is a process and not an event.

Discussion Questions:

1. Do you relate to the two stories at the beginning of the chapter - one with a four-year-old son hitting his two-year-old sister, and the other one with a teenager coming home late? In what ways? If not, in what ways?

2. How does the gospel of Jesus Christ provide the ultimate model of what God has called us to as parents in terms of working change into our lives as his children?

"[T]he Father's work of justification is an event, but his work of transformation is literally a life-long process. When justifying you, God is fully aware that he is committing himself to a day-by-day process of illumining, confronting, convicting, forgiving, transforming, and delivering grace" (p. 87).

3. Think about when you had a confrontation with your children because of your short-term, event view of parenting rather than the long-term, life-long process view. Can you share what happened

with the group? How might it have been different if you had the long-term view instead?

Parenting is not a series of dramatic confrontation-confession events, but rather a life-long process of incremental awareness and progressive change. The four-year-old will not say after you confront him, "I am a self-centered, self-ruling idolater in need of redemption." The middle schooler will not become a fully transformed human being and the teenager will still need your parenting wisdom. I think that the desire for overnight change gets us into trouble" (p. 87).

The Blind Leading the Blind

4. Which is more challenging to you: that your children are selfish and rebellious or that they are blind to the fact that they are selfish and rebellious?

5. How is spiritual blindness different from physical blindness? When have you noticed that your children are spiritually blind?

"Unlike physical blindness, where you know you are blind, spiritually blind people are blind to their blindness. They are blind, but they think they see quite well. Spiritual blindness happens at the intersection of the deceptiveness of sin and the delusion of self-knowledge. Both of these are operating in the hearts of all of our children. They are not just misbehaving; they

are blind to their misbehavior and the sin of their hearts that creates it. Understanding this alters the way we need to think about the parenting process" (p. 89-90).

6. When have you noticed that you are spiritually blind? How have you opened your eyes to your own spiritual blindness to the degree that you're aware now? Did it happen through one dramatic event or has it been a life-long process for you?

"Like our children, we are in need of a Father who will patiently work over a long period of time to help us to see. We need a Father who, in mercy, will not demand instantaneous change. We need a Father who understands our condition and confronts us not just with his rebuke, but with his grace. And although you are an adult and have perhaps known God for years, you still have pockets of spiritual blindness in you and you still tend to resist the care that you yet need. Like our children, you and I do the same wrong things over and over again because we are not only blind, but we are blind to our blindness. We need compassionate, patient care if we are ever going to change, and so do our children" (p. 90-91).

Parenting, the Never-Ending Conversation

- Three mentalities that need to shape your parenting:
    1) You need to parent with a process mentality.

    2) You need to see parenting as one unending

PARENTING DISCUSSION GUIDE

conversation

3) You need to parent with a project mentality

7. Reflect again on your answers to Question 3. If you had the process mentality when you had the confrontation with your child, knowing that parenting is a bit-by-bit, piece-by-piece, lifelong, connected process where you can't look for a dramatic transformational conclusion to your encounters with your child, how would you have handled the situation differently?

8. How would seeing parenting as one unending conversation be freeing to you?

9. What does it mean to parent with a sense of project rather than being reactive as a parent? Have you spotted your children being *"emotional weathermen"*?

Following the Father

10. According to Tripp, what gets in the way of good parenting? How come?

    1) A lack of opportunity

    2) The character of your child

    3) The character of the parent

11. Good parenting takes patience, humility, self-control, submission, gentleness, love, faithfulness, and joy (p.94). How do

you feel when you see this list of character qualities?

"[T]he good news is that the message of the Bible isn't that God puts an undoable standard before us and then sits by and judges us for our failures. No, the message is that God puts an uncompromising standard before us, then sends his Son to perfectly meet that standard on our behalf, so that we can be free to admit our failures and go to God for help. The cross of Jesus Christ means I don't have to deny my struggle as a parent, I don't have to act as if I'm something that I'm not, and I surely don't have to hide from the only One who is able to help me" (p.95-95).

12. God blesses us not only with forgiveness but also with new potential. How has God blessed you with his transforming grace to do his work of change within you in your life so far?

"Like your children, you aren't left to parent yourself because God daily blesses you with his presence and grace, so that you can pass that same grace on to your children. Like you, they need to come to confess that they don't measure up. And because they don't measure up, they not only need your parental care, but even more importantly, they need the heavenly Father's life-long and heart-changing agenda of mercy" (p.96).

PARENTING DISCUSSION GUIDE

Chapter 7 - Lost

Principle: As a parent you're not dealing just with bad behavior, but a condition that causes bad behavior.

Discussion Questions:

1. Have you been exhausted and discouraged trying to deal with your child's behavior? What happened? Why was your child having a bad behavior?

"Our children are not just disobedient; they are disobedient because they are lost. Our children do not just make foolish choices; they make foolish choices because they are lost. Our children do not just have trouble getting along with their siblings; they have trouble getting along with their siblings because they are lost. Our children are not just lazy; they are lazy because they are lost. Our children don't just resist our authority; they resist our authority because they are lost. Everything that we're dealing with is the result of something deeper that must be in our understanding and focus" (pp. 98-99).

Three Days of Good Behavior

PARENTING DISCUSSION GUIDE

2. What are the risks of parents caring only about their children's behavior and not looking deeper into what goes on in their hearts?

Your Children Are Lost. What Does That Mean?

3. Sheep need a shepherd, are prone to wander, and are incapable of rescuing themselves when they wandered. How are your children like sheep? What one or two specific things can you do to be more faithful in God's calling of you to shepherd your children in their lostness?

4. What can parents learn from the parable of the lost coin in terms of the attitude toward their children who are lost?

"These three verses portray with power the compassion, the patience, and the grace that we are called to represent as God's ambassadors in the lives of our children. We're not mad at them because they're lost and need our help. We don't push their lostness in their faces. We don't remind them how much more righteous we are than they are, and that we would have never thought of doing and saying the things they do and say. No, we parent with mercy and grace. We live with them with patient hearts, and we celebrate every time they confess or choose to do what is right" (p.104).

5. What are the two dangers inside every child that the parable of the lost son reveals? (p.105)

6. If the rescue your children need is rescue from themselves because of the susceptibility to temptation and the tendency toward self-deception, what might be an effective parenting approach that truly helps children to be rescued from themselves?

"[Authority, rules, enforcement of the rules, accountability] are important for protecting a child from himself, but they have no power whatsoever to deliver a child from himself, and every child needs that deliverance. Like the lost son, lost children need compassion, lost children need understanding, lost children need patience, lost children need acceptance, lost children need forgiveness, lost children need grace. It is stirring to see that the father of the lost son never gave up, he never gave way to bitterness and anger, he never threw away his hope, he never closed the door of his heart, and he never quit loving his son. He longed for and looked for and was ready for his son's return" (pp. 105-106).

Two Big Lies Every Lost Child Believes

7. What are the two big lies every lost child believes? Can you describe what they look like in your or other childrens' lives? How about in your life when you were little or younger?

So What Do Lost Children Need?

Lost children need:

PARENTING DISCUSSION GUIDE

- Insight: not just to be told what to do but also to be enabled to see their lostness
- Compassion: not being irritated by their lostness but mourning it and longing for them to be found
- Hope: being assured that help is available in their lostness
- Rescue: not a behavior-control mission but a heart-rescue mission, looking for every opportunity to address heart issues
- Wisdom: knowing when to say no, especially to themselves

8. Which of these needs do your children need the most? What specific things can you start doing this week to provide them with what they need in their heart-rescue mission?

"So parents, what's the bottom line? Well, as Jesus came to seek and to save those who are lost, he calls us to love and to rescue our lost children. We don't give way to irritation, frustration, impatience, or discouragement. We move toward our children with the grace of forgiveness, wisdom, correction, and rescue, and we pray every day that God will empower our work as parents, and that he will change our children at that deepest of levels where every human being, including us, needs to be changed" (p. 110).

Chapter 8 - Authority

Principle: One of the foundational heart issues in the life of every child is authority. Teaching and modeling the protective beauty of authority is one of the foundations of good parenting.

Discussion Questions:

1. "I have a four-year-old son who I cannot control." What do you feel when you hear this sentence?

The Central Issue

2. "[T]here is no more important heart issue for every child ever born than the issue of authority" (p.113). Do you agree or disagree? Why?

"Why is this so important? Because submission to authority that is not me is unnatural for any sinner. Sin makes us want our own way. Sin makes us want to set our own rules. Sin convinces all of us that we know better. Sin causes me to want to do what I want to do when and how I want to do it. Sin makes me resist being told what to do by another. Sin really does insert me in the center of my world, the one place that I must never be because it is the place for God and God alone" (p.113).

3. What surface issues often create tension and struggle between you and your children? Have you considered that the deeper issue beneath the surface issues is your child's bondage to himself, sin-induced drive and determination for self-rule, and natural resistance to authority?

4. What resources do you have as a Christian parent in dealing with your children's addiction to self-rule?

"Mom and Dad, you have no ability at all—by the tone of your voice, by the force of your personality, by your physical size, or by your threats—to deliver your children from their addiction to self-rule. If you had that power, Jesus and his work would not have been necessary. But Jesus does have the power" (p.114-115).

The Gospel of Jesus Christ and Authority

5. *"Exercising ambassadorial authority is doing gospel work"* (p.115). What does it mean that God makes his invisible authority visible by sending visible authority figures as his representatives? What kind of picture are your children getting of God's authority by the way you exercise yours?

6. *"Helping your children to understand why they do what they do is doing gospel work"* (p.117). How often do you combine moments of discipline with patient, insight-giving instruction?

7. *"Establishing authority early in little things is doing gospel work"* (p.118). Did you fight or are you fighting your authority battles early? If not, what changes in the way you look at little moments of discipline need to take place in you and the way you respond to your children?

8. *"Exercising consistent authority is doing gospel work"* (p.120). Is your exercise of parental authority consistent because it's driven by God's call or is it inconsistent because it's shaped by the emotion of the moment?

9. *"Confessing that when it comes to authority you are more like your children than unlike them is doing gospel work"* (p.121). happen. Do you humbly own the rebellion of your own heart as you deal with the rebellion of your children in a way that causes you to exercise authority with patience and grace?

10. *"In discussions of authority, talking about the cross of Jesus Christ is doing gospel work"* (p.121). In moments of discipline, do you often point your children to the hope and help that is to be found in the life, death, and resurrection of Jesus?

"It really is true that there is no more central issue in the lives of our children. Their struggle with authority really does reveal the depth of the hold of sin on their hearts and their need for the grace of the Savior. And in that way we really are like our children. When we admit that, we are able to exercise authority with humility and grace, giving our children a little picture of

how gloriously beautiful and good God's authority actually is" (p.122).

Chapter 9 - Foolishness

Principle: The foolishness inside your children is more dangerous to them than the temptation outside of them. Only God's grace has the power to rescue fools.

Discussion Questions:

1. What is foolishness? When do you see foolishness at work in the lives of others, of your children, and of yourself?

It's All about the Heart

2. Proverbs 4:23 says, "Keep your heart with all vigilance, for from it flow the springs of life." What do you think this verse means? Why is this important in parenting?

3. How often do you talk about your children's heart at the moments of discipline and correction, what Tripp calls "grace" moments? Can you share some examples of utilizing "grace" moments to join God's transforming work within our children?

"If parenting must include and focus on the heart, ... First, you must remind yourself again and again, so that in the press of the duties of parenting you don't forget that all of your children's behavior problems are heart problems. ... The second

thing you must call yourself to remember is that lasting change in the behavior of your children ... will always travel through the pathway of the heart. If the heart of your child does not change, his behavior won't change for very long. This means that every moment of discipline and correction must be accompanied with instruction ... In these moments ask questions, tell stories, give illustrations—anything you can do to get the child to step out of himself, to quit defending himself, and to look into and examine his heart." (p.126-127).*

4. Could your parenting (or a part of it) be described as *monastic* parenting? In what ways? Why is monastic parenting inadequate?

"I will give you a new heart, and a new spirit I will put in you. And I will remove the heart of stone from your flesh and give you a heart of flesh" (Ezek. 36:26).

If the Heart Is the Problem, Then What Is the Problem with the Heart?

5. What does the Bible say about foolishness, especially in Psalm 53:1-3? What implication does it have for parenting?

Tripp uses four words to answer the question, "What does it look like to be visible extenders of God's invisible grace in the lives of our children?" (p.132)

6. *Glory:* The only solution to your child's addiction to his own

glory is to introduce him to a greater glory. ... Our job as a parent is to open the eyes of our children to the stunning glory of God. Are you capturing these glory moments with a mission to rescue your children from their foolishness? (p.133)

7. *Wisdom*: A fool needs wisdom, God's wisdom and his wise ways. Do you have experiences of not just enforcing the rules but also talking about how gorgeous God's wise ways are with your children? How can you do this more often and effectively?

8. *Story*: Do you tell the story of the person and work of Jesus to your children, the story of how God in his mercy and wisdom rescues fools? Does the way you give instruction (not just the content of your instruction) during the moments of discipline reflect this story of the gospel of grace?

9. *Welcome*. Do you talk about how God, "right here, right now, extends a welcome to them to confess their foolishness, to seek his forgiveness, and to receive his eternal help"? (p.134) What is one tangible and specific thing you can do in your next moment of discipline to be a visible representative of the patient and forgiving welcome that God extends to all who come to him?

10. Have you been a fool, turning moments of ministry into moments of anger, personalizing what is not personal, settling for quick solutions that do not get to the heart of the matter? Why does God send fools (parents) to be used as tools of rescuing fools (children)?

"The mystery of the way God works is that he sends fools to rescue fools and because he does, it takes grace to be a tool of God's agenda of rescuing grace. Parents, the more you are ready and willing to confess the foolishness that causes you to need God's grace, the more you will be willing and ready to extend that grace to the foolish hearts of the children he has entrusted to your care. But remember: because of what Jesus has done for us, that grace is ready for the taking right here, right now" (p.136).

Chapter 10 - Character

Principle: Not all of the wrong your children do is a direct rebellion to authority; much of the wrong is the result of a lack of character.

Discussion Questions:

1. How often do you think about the character development of your children? How important is it in your parenting?

"[I]f you deal with a lack of character with a lack of character, you will not accomplish what God has given you to accomplish in the hearts of your children. Proper handling of these kinds of situations always begins not with a lecture, but with confession. Before you talk to your children, you and I need to talk to ourselves and to our Lord. We need to confess that it's not just our children who lack character; we do as well" (p.139).

2. How does recognizing God's patience, kindness, and grace in the on-going character development of your heart empower you in your parenting?

A Stunning Connection

3. What is the most significant of all human functions that the Bible (Romans 1) connects character issues to? Can you explain how?

"The character issues in the lives of your children exist not just because they want bad things, but because they become enslaved to good things. You see, a desire for even a good thing really does become a bad thing when it becomes a ruling thing" (p.142-143).

4. Do you know the objects of your children's worship? The idols of their hearts they tend to fall into? Do you intentionally make connections between their character issues and the idols of their hearts and help them see for themselves?

"Sally doesn't understand why she's feeling what she's feeling and doing what she's doing because she doesn't understand the connection between character and worship. Sally needs something more than a parent who will say a firm no; Sally needs a parent who will help Sally understand what's in her heart and how it shapes the way she responds to her mom. These are not the hard moments of parenting; these are wonderful moments where eye-opening and heart-changing conversations are given an opportunity to happen" (p.145).

5. How can the costly atoning sacrificial love and grace of parents toward their children melt their hearts to admit their conditions

within and see the connection between character and worship in their hearts?

"No one has ever learned that he or she is a sinner by being told that they are." - Tim Keller

A Descriptive List

Envy. How often do you have to deal with the conflict that results because one sibling is jealous of another?

Strife. Is there ever a day when you don't have to deal with some kind of problem between your children?

Deceit. How often are our children less-than-honest about what they have said or done?

Gossip. Do you not find your children being regularly seduced by the temptation to talk negatively about someone to someone else?

Insolent. To be insolent is to be rude and unmannerly. What parent doesn't have to deal with this on a regular basis?

Haughty. It's the pride in the hearts of our children that again and again makes parenting them difficult.

Boastful. Boastfulness is pride with an open mouth. Our children are way too comfortable with announcing that they are better, smarter, prettier, faster, stronger, more likeable, etc. Foolish. There is never a day when somehow, someway you are not confronted with the foolishness of one of your children.

PARENTING DISCUSSION GUIDE

Heartless. It is sad to see how heartless our children can be in their responses to one another" (p.145-146).

6. How does the list above help us see the connection between worship and character? Does it help you see the connection between worship and character in your children's hearts?

"Your children don't so much need character management *as they need* worship realignment. *They don't first have a character problem; they have a worship problem that produces a character problem. Because of this they need more than character critique; they need to be given insight into the worship function of their hearts and how it shapes the way they react in the relationships and situations of their daily lives. They really do need truth that has the power to set them free" (p.146).*

7. How much are you aware of your own character issues and their connections to the idols of your heart? How often do you confess your need for patient parenting care by your Father God so that your children can learn to do the same?

"[God] works on the character of your heart as well, so that you progressively become what he designed you to be. Because he is committed to character change, your Lord goes after the idols of your heart and he will not rest until every thought, desire, choice, word, and action is fully rooted in the worship of him.

You and I are still blessed every day with his fatherly care because the war of worship still rages in our hearts. Now God calls you to do with your children what he graciously does with you every day" (p.146-147).

Bobby's Story

8. Bobby said to Tripp that no one ever talked to him about what rules his heart until he was thirty-five years old even though he grew up in a Christian home. Imagine your children saying the same thing when they become thirty-five. What are some practical small steps you can take this week to avoid that imaginary scenario becoming real?

PARENTING DISCUSSION GUIDE

Chapter 11 - False Gods

Principle: You are parenting a worshiper, so it's important to remember that what rules your child's heart will control his behavior.

Discussion Questions:

1. What score would you give yourself on how well or poorly you would answer these questions (1 being very poorly and 10 being very well)? - Why do my children do the things they do? How does change take place in children's hearts and lives? How can I be a tool of change in the hearts and lives of my children?

"Why have I started with these three questions? Because the answer to these questions is found in a single word: worship. *Every single thing your child has ever said or done is rooted in worship"* (p.150).

What Is Worship?

2. What is worship? Why is it something everyone does every day? Do you agree?

3. What were our children made for, ultimately? How is this reflected in your parenting?

4. When was the last time you considered your children's capacity to worship when you noticed bad behaviour in their lives?

"As a parent you have to look through the lens of the truth that your children are worshipers in order to understand and deal with all that is going on in your children's lives. God will use the normal stuff of daily responsibilities, opportunities, relationships, and temptations to expose to you what is going on in the heart of the worshipers that have been entrusted to your care. He will do this again and again, because he is a God of gloriously zealous and patient grace. He is after the heart of your child even when you don't have the sight or the sense to be. And he will be faithful to give you opportunities to see and help your children to see the God-replacements that are progressively gaining control of their thoughts, desires, feelings, choices, hopes, dreams, cravings, values, and goals. He is on a mission of rescue, and he has appointed you to be his representative on-site in the lives of your children. For a parent, there is no biblical observation, no parental job description, and no daily goal more important than what we are talking about right now" (p.158).

5. What right now does God want your child to see that he/she is not now seeing and how can you help him/her see it?

6. How can parents lead children to confession? What does it look

PARENTING DISCUSSION GUIDE

like? Do you have an example (whether from your experience or someone else) you can share?

7. "To say your children are worshipers means you have no power to free them from their biggest problem" (p.161). Do you agree or disagree? Why or why not?

"Admitting our inability is not giving up as a parent. On the contrary, this humble admission is the soil in which effective, Christ-centered, grace-driven, hope-infused, and heart-changing parenting grows. If you confess your inability, then you do not allow yourself to think that a louder voice, more graphic vocabulary, or a bigger threat is going to alter the worship content of your child's heart. What our children need is the rescue of divine insight, divine conviction, and a divine commitment to change" (p.161).

8. "Because your children are worshipers, your only hope for them is the grace of the Lord Jesus Christ" (p.161), and this doesn't mean that we do nothing. Which of the things parents are to do as sharp tools of God mentioned below do you feel you need to do more in your parenting?

    1) Faithfully hold God's high standard before children

    2) Lovingly confront their wrong choices and actions

    3) Work to help give them insight into their hearts

    4) Be humbly honest about my own heart struggles

PARENTING DISCUSSION GUIDE

5) Talk to them again and again about the grace to be found in Christ Jesus

6) Model God's patience and forgiveness

7) Do all of the above again and again because I believe the Saviour is in me, with me, and for me

8) Believe God is for my children because he has graciously placed them in a family of faith

9. Why is it important to remember that "we are more like our children than unlike them"?

"Parenting is being willing to expend your time, gifts, energies, and resources in a daily battle of worship as God's tool in the lives of your children. It's never just about food, friends, Facebook, homework, sleep-time, clothes, household rules, or sibling squabbles. Those things are struggles because there is a deeper war going on inside the hearts of your children. Every struggle in these areas is an opportunity that is given to you by a God of amazing grace to get at those deeper issues for the sake of the redemption, rescue, and transformation of your children. And God will give you everything you need to engage yourself in that deeper war" (p.162).

Chapter 12 - Control

Principle: The goal of parenting is not control of behavior, but rather heart and life change.

Discussion Questions:

1. At the beginning of the chapter, there are twelve little vignettes of different parents trying to control the behaviors of a child or the results of those attempts. Which story do you relate to the most? Or if you don't relate to any of them, what are some of your own ways of trying to control your child's behaviors?

What Our Children Need

2. It's a good thing to exercise faithful control over children to fill their needs of guidance, protection, instruction, wisdom, authority, rules, structure, preparation, understanding, confrontation, discipline, warning, love, forgiveness, and security (pp.166-169). What is missing in this list?

"He calls you to exercise faithful control, but never to be satisfied with the fact that you have. Your dear children desperately need your parental control, but they will not be all God has designed them to be if that's all that you give them" (p.170).

PARENTING DISCUSSION GUIDE

Every Child's Deeper Need

1) Your Children Need to See Their Sin, So They'll Cry Out for God's Mercy

3. Read Psalm 51:1-2. Have you ever made this cry before God? Has your child made this cry? When does crying out for God's mercy happen? How can we lovingly and patiently bring our children to the point where they too cry out for God's mercy?

2) Your Children Need to Understand the Nature of Sin, So They Don't Minimize Its Danger (vv. 1–3)

4. When was the last time you warned your children about something dangerous around them that they need to be aware of and avoid? Do you ever warn them about their sin?

"There is no more harmful thing in a child's life than his own sin. To be made aware of it and its power to destroy is a good and loving thing" (p.173).

5. In Psalm 51, David uses three words to describe sin and its life-crushing danger. What are they and what do they mean? How are you helping your children to acknowledge the danger of sin living inside their hearts?

"If your children are going to come to the place where they fear the sin that is inside them and seek God's help and yours, they will need to understand the gravity of sin" (p175).

3) Your Children Need to Understand That Their Problem Is Not with Their Parents, but with God (v. 4)

6. Do you agree that every sin is vertical, a fist in the face of God, a desire to remove God from his throne and sit there yourself? Why or why not?

"As a parent, you must always remember the verticality of the wrong that your children do and not make it just about you. But you must also help them to understand that they were made for God, created to do his will, and because this is so, every wrong thing they do is done against him" (p.176).

4) Your Children Need to Understand That Sin Is a Nature Problem That Produces Behavior Problems (v. 5)

7. Have you ever helped your children understand that they don't simply sin but they *are* sinners? Can you share some specific examples?

"It is loving to help your children to understand that it's not enough to confess that they sometimes do what is wrong. They need to come to the place where they confess that wrong lives inside them, and because of that they are in desperate need of God's rescuing, forgiving, transforming, and delivering mercy" (p.176).

PARENTING DISCUSSION GUIDE

5) Your Children Need to Understand That Since Sin Is a Heart Problem, the Only Solution Is a New Heart (v. 10)

8. When do you recognize your child's need for a new heart? In what ways do your children try to manage their heart problem rather than seeking a divine heart transplant? What can you do differently next time to help your children acknowledge their need for divine surgery?

6) Your Children Need to Be Taught to Run to the Only Place of Hope: The Forgiving Grace of God (v. 14)

9. If "the doorway to hope is hopelessness" (p.178), how do we bring our children to that wholesome and heart-changing place of personal hopelessness? What makes it a process of patient and loving rescue rather than of condemnation?

"You are called to make use of every opportunity that God will give you to help your children to become aware of the grave danger of the sin that lives inside them. You don't do this with irritation or impatience, but with grace, acknowledging that you are just like them, a person in need of God's mercy. Self-righteously pointing out the sin of others never works; it is offensive and condescending, and it will close down the hearts of your children. Ask God to give you the grace to come to them to talk to them about their sin as a person who is much more grieved by the sin that is inside you than the sin that is in them. When you come this way, your tenderness and humility becomes a workroom for God to do in the heart of your child what you can't do" (p.178).

Chapter 13 - Rest

Principle: It is only rest in God's presence and grace that will make you a joyful and patient parent.

Discussion Questions:

1. Do you feel exhausted, discouraged, overwhelmed, or lacking rest in your life of parenting today? If yes, how do you think you have lost a sense of rest in your heart?

"Yes, as a parent, he had called me to do things that were way beyond my natural abilities, character, wisdom, strength, and gifts, but he had never sent me out to do them **alone***. Aloneness is a cruel lie that will defeat us every time. So I want to help you to remember and in remembering to rest. It is a heart at rest that will enable you to do the good things that God has called every parent to do"* (p.182).

The Best Parenting Passage in the Entire Bible

2. What has been the most helpful Bible passage for you as a parent? Why?

PARENTING DISCUSSION GUIDE

<u>Matthew 28:18-20</u>

And Jesus came and said to them, "All authority in heaven and on earth has been given to me. Go therefore and make disciples of all nations, baptizing them in the name of the Father and of the Son and of the Holy Spirit, teaching them to observe all that I have commanded you. And behold I am with you always, to the end of the age."

3. In light of the passage above, what is the core mission of parents?

4. Are you working to be used of God to make disciples of your children? Reflecting on your life as a parent (think of your last couple of weeks), how important is this calling to you compared to other tasks you're committed to as a parent?

5. What does it mean that as a parent you are called to teach your children to observe everything that Jesus has commanded?

"Our children must learn to look at life through the lens of the will and plan of their Creator. What we are talking about is helping them to develop a comprehensive biblical worldview that is a way of looking at life that is distinctively God-centered and biblically driven" (p.185).

6. Have you tried to disciple your children so that they observe everything Jesus has commanded? How hard or easy is it?

"Our passage makes it very clear that Jesus would not ever call you to this huge parenting task without also blessing you with his mind-blowing promises as well. If you understand and embrace his promises, then you can give yourself to participate in what is impossible for you to produce and not have discouraging or even paralyzing anxiety in your heart. In fact, good, loving, faithful, grace-driven parents only ever grow in the soil of a heart at rest. Jesus's promises are not so much promises, but reminders of the unshakable identity of every one of his children. The two promises here are meant to remind you of what the great heavenly Father has become for you by grace. These promises define for you not only who God is, but who you are as his child" (p. 186).

7. How do Jesus's words, "all authority in heaven and earth has been given to me," comfort us? If this is true, how might you look at your life differently today as a parent?

8. How about these words of Jesus, "And behold, I am with you always, to the end of the age"?

"This means that in every moment when you are parenting, you are being parented. In every moment when you are called to give grace, you are being given grace. In every moment when you are rescuing and protecting your children, you are being rescued and protected. In every moment when you feel alone, you are anything but alone because he goes wherever you go. It is impossible for your parenting to ever wander outside the light of

his presence. He never forgets you, he never turns his back on you, he never wanders away for a moment, he never favors someone else over you, he never gets mad and refuses to be with you, he never grows cynical, he will never give up, and he will never ever quit. He is tenderly, patiently, faithfully, and eternally with you. You can bank on his care. You can rest in his presence" (pp. 187-188).

9. The practical meanings of hoping in the two redemptive realities (promises) of the Great Commission are stated below. Which one do you find to be the most helpful to you and why? Which one do you need now?

1) *You will not be punished for your failure*; you will fail, but you can always run to God for help and receive his forgiveness and help.

2) *You are welcomed by grace to new beginnings*; you are free from living in the regret of things done wrong, and you can commit to new and better things today.

3) *You are not left to your limited resources*; God's power, wisdom, and character will enable, direct, and redirect you with his infinite resources.

4) *God blesses you with the right here, right now wisdom of his Word*; God's redemptive story in the Bible gives you wisdom to deal

with everything you face in life.

5) *You do not have to load the burden of your children's welfare on your shoulders every morning*; the burden rests on the shoulders of the One who sent you. And his shoulders are big enough.

6) *God will never close his ears to your cries for help*; whenever you run to God in your need, he will pay careful attention to your cries.

7) *Weakness is not a curse; it's a blessing*; God says, "My grace is sufficient for you, for my power is made perfect in weakness" (2 Cor. 12:9).

8) *Success is about faithfulness, not results*; God would never call you to produce what you can't produce. He simply calls you to be faithful.

10. How can you remind yourself of these truths so that you can maintain rest in your heart? What are some simple things you can do with one another in this group regularly to help each other rest in God's faithfulness and promises?

"It really is true that good, godly, transformative parenting grows best in the soil of a heart at rest. Parent, is your heart at rest? Is your parenting fueled by trust? Or does worry haunt your heart? You have reason for rest. You have been sent, but

the One who sent you rules every location and relationship he sends you to. You have been sent, but the One who sent you has packed up and come with you, so that you would have everything you need to do what he's called you to do. Fight the assessment that the job is too big. Fight the feeling that you are all alone. Meditate upon and celebrate his power and presence and go do what you've been chosen to do with courage and hope" (p. 194).

Chapter 14 - Mercy

Principle: No parent gives mercy better than one who is convinced that he desperately needs it himself.

Discussion Questions:

1. When was the last time you needed God's mercy? How often do you need God's mercy?

2. Describe a time when you received mercy from someone. How did you feel? Were you changed by it? If yes, how?

3. Why do you think it is hard to give or receive mercy sometimes?

"There is not a day when your children do not need your mercy. Because of this, your primary calling as a parent is not first to represent God's judgment, but rather to constantly deliver his mercy" (p.195).

Mercy Requires Mercy

4. Who gives mercy best?

PARENTING DISCUSSION GUIDE

"You see, if you forget who you are and what you need, it becomes easier to parent your children without mercy. Think about how amazing God's plan is! God uses the needs of our children to expose how needy we are as their parents, so that we would do all that we do toward them with sympathetic and understanding hearts. God is working on you through your children, so that he can work through you for your children" (p.199).

5. What might be one need in you as a parent that God is exposing through your children these days?

Responses of Mercy

6. Tripp says that God called you as a parent to be his first responders in the lives of your children on your missions of mercy. What might this mean in terms of the way you respond to your children in your everyday life?

7. Below are what parenting as a lifelong mission of mercy looks like. Which do you find to be the most helpful to you and why? What practical steps can you take this week to live out your mission of mercy?

> 1) *Look for every opportunity to shower your children with grace;* the law alone does not have the power to rescue and transform your child, but grace can.

2) *Be careful to help your children see the heart behind the behavior;* ask them about their thoughts, feelings, and desires to help them examine their hearts, over and over again.

3) *Be patiently committed to the process;* the mission of mercy is seldom an event and almost always an extended process. Be patiently willing to have similar heart conversations again and again.

4) *Point your kids every day to Jesus;* introduce your children to him early in their lives and look for opportunities every day to talk about his wisdom, power, sovereignty, love, and grace. Talk about the why and how of Jesus' salvation. Connect the gospel to your life and their lives.

5) *Humbly accept your limits;* you can't change your children by yelling, by threat, guilt, or manipulation, by anger, by punishments, or by shaming and name-calling. Only God can. You are freed from the burden of changing your children.

6) *Remind your heart each morning to rest in the presence and power of your heavenly Father;* through it's more natural to worry than to trust God, take a moment to remember and rest and then go out and parent with a heart filled with hope, courage, and love from your Father God.

7) *Willingly confess your faults;* you're also in the long process of change, not just your children. Let Jesus be your advocate and be free to confess without fear of God's rejection. Help your children seek God's help by seeking God's help yourself, first.

PARENTING DISCUSSION GUIDE

8) *Root all that you require, say, and do in the wonderful wisdom of Scripture;* your job is to be God's tool for the purpose of forming the image of God's Son in your children, and the Bible is your primary tool. Love Scripture enough to be able to teach your children the depth and width of the glorious gospel and God's grand story and plan of saving humanity and all creation.

9) *Don't treat opportunities like hassles;* your best opportunities to get at issues of the heart in your children will come unexpectedly. Resist turning a moment of ministry into a moment of anger.

10) *Be slow to anger and quick to forgive;* seek God's help and commit to resisting anger. Address and work on your anger. Come up with ways to deal with your anger at the moment in your responses to your children.

11) *Pray before, during, and after;* pray constantly, recognizing God's position, admitting your need, and surrendering to God's plan.

12) *Do all of these things over and over again;* Parenting is about the willingness to live a life of long-term, intentional repetition. God has called you to a life of patient perseverance. He's called you to be his tool of grace again and again and again.

"[God] blesses you with his presence, power, wisdom, and grace. He faithfully parents you, so that by his faithful grace you can faithfully parent your children. In every moment of parenting,

the wise heavenly Father is working on everybody in the room. You are blessed to be chosen to go on the mission of missions, and you are blessed with his grace so that every day your parenting would be dyed with the most powerful force of change in the universe: mercy" (pp.208-209).

About the Author

Andrew Yoon Joo Lee is a missionary to international students in South Korea. He was born in Seoul, South Korea and moved to the United States to study abroad when he was fifteen years old. He educated at Johns Hopkins University, started his Master of Divinity at Gordon-Conwell Theological Seminary, and finished it at Regent College. When he lived in Coquitlam, BC, Canada with his wife, Irene, he served as the youth ministry director at Nelson Avenue Community Church and ministered to international students at Douglas College through International Student Ministries Canada (ISMC). In 2022, Andrew and Irene moved back to Korea where Andrew continues to serve international students as a missionary sent by ISMC and Resonate Global Mission (Christian Reformed Church). He is also passionate about living missionally in the neighborhood, small group ministry and missional communities, and business as mission which all stem from Missio Deo, God's mission of restoring all creation into shalom.

Made in the USA
Las Vegas, NV
23 December 2023